Mice as a Hobby

by Jack Young

SAVE-OUR-PLANET SERIES

T.F.H. Publications, Inc.

Contents

Distributed in the UNITED STATES to the Pet Trade by T.F.H. Publications, Inc., One T.F.H. Plaza, Neptune City, NJ 07753; distributed in the UNITED STATES to the Bookstore and Library Trade by National Book Network, Inc. 4720 Boston Way, Lanham MD 20706; in CANADA to the Pet Trade by H & L Pet Supplies Inc., 27 Kingston Crescent, Kitchener, Ontario N2B 2T6; Rolf C. Hagen Ltd., 3225 Sartelon Street, Montreal 382 Quebec; in CANADA to the Book Trade by Macmillan of Canada (A Division of Canada Publishing Corporation), 164 Commander Boulevard, Agincourt, Ontario M1S 3C7; in ENGLAND by T.F.H. Publications, PO Box 15, Waterlooville PO7 6BQ; in AUSTRALIA AND THE SOUTH PACIFIC by T.F.H. (Australia), Pty. Ltd., Box 149, Brookvale 2100 N.S.W., Australia; in NEW ZEALAND by Brooklands Aquarium Ltd., 5 McGiven Drive, New Plymouth, RD1 New Zealand; in the PHILIPPINES by Bio-Research, 5 Lippay Street, San Lorenzo Village, Makati, Rizal; in SOUTH AFRICA by Multipet Pty. Ltd., P.O. Box 35347, Northway, 4065, South Africa. Published by T.F.H. Publications, Inc. Manufactured in the United States of America by T.F.H. Publications, Inc.

Introduction

The little house mouse, *Mus musculus*, is probably one critter that needs no introduction to anyone. Its fame is worldwide, and its association with humans goes back to the very dawn of history. However, a little

The mouse is different things to different people. To young children it is both good and bad, the former in the shape of Mickey Mouse, or the country mice of Beatrix Potter, the latter as the creature of the dark seen in movies scurrying in drains and chasing terrified children and old folks alike. To the scientist it is a laboratory

background history will be of benefit to those who may wish to keep one or two mice as pets or to take up breeding them as a hobby.

animal that provides a constant source of information, while to the zoologist it is both a fascinating creature to study and the most readily available source of food for reptiles, amphibians, and raptors kept in zoological collections.

The common little house mouse played its part in the largest mass death of us humans—the Black Plague of Europe that killed millions of people in medieval times. It has been the source of cult worship and has, throughout our history, greatly influenced the economies of entire civilizations. Mice can eat their way through millions of tons of grain crops in a year, so it is no surprise to find that these little

A long-haired pied mouse. Photo by Horst Bielfeld.

A hand-tame pet mouse. Photo by Michael Gilroy.

rodents have been the target of government attempts to control them. The Egyptians found that cats were the best controllers of mice, thus the arrival of these efficient predators came as a direct result of the mouse's activities.

We have tried to poison them out of existence, trap them, burn them, and hunt them—but all to no avail. Wherever humans decide to settle, so will they inherit an attendant mouse population. So versatile are mice that colonies of them have been found living in carcasses of meat in sub-zero cold stores. They had developed extra fat layers, grew thicker and longer coats—and of course had a readily available food supply in the form of the meat.

For many centuries, indeed until very recent times, the mouse was used as one of numerous ingredients in potions and lotions believed to cure all manner of problems from diseases and lumps, to infertility and cataracts.

THE MOUSE AS A PET

Given all of the negative aspects of the mouse, it might be pondered why anyone would wish to keep them as pets. Most mothers are terrified at the thought of pet mice getting loose and scurrying around the home, so let us remove the prejudices of centuries that shape our thoughts and look at the virtues of mice as pets. For one thing, they are small, an obvious advantage; they are quiet, their squeak hardly being comparable to the raucous screeching of some parrots, or the constant barking and howling of some dogs.

They are extremely clean little creatures that fastidiously groom themselves. They are almost odorless, (the male being less so than the female) so any smells from them will be the result of poor hygiene on behalf of their owner. They never bite unless provoked by bad handling, and they are very intelligent animals for their diminutive size. This makes them

A pied cream mouse, one of the many attractive color varieties of the domestic mouse. Photo by Michael Gilroy.

A harvest mouse ascends a seedhead. This is one of the most abundant wild rodents of Europe.

interesting to observe. They are fascinating animals from a color-breeding viewpoint because of their

mice is quite low, and their upkeep is likewise reasonable. All in all they are ideal little pets and can teach children much about the responsibility of caring for a living creature.

You should make a clear distinction in your mind between the pet fancy mouse and its wild ancestors. Pet mice are the result of hundreds of generations of mice that have been selectively bred to be placid. They do not carry all manner of diseases, and their chances of surviving in the wild, should they ever escape, are slim. They would be attacked by wild mice and would quickly be caught by the many

reproductive rate, and they are excellent pets to exhibit. The initial cost of pet natural predators of their family—cats, snakes, weasels, ferrets, and birds of prey. Fancy mice have become fully domesticated just the same as rabbits, guinea pigs, cats and dogs.

MOUSE CLASSIFICATION

The mouse is a member of the highly successful group of animals known as rodents, which are placed by taxonomists in the order Rodentia. The main feature of these animals is their gnawing front teeth, which grow throughout their lives. These teeth are called incisors and are paired (two in each jaw). Behind the incisors there are no canine teeth, as in cats, dogs, and primates, but a gap called a diastema. This enables rodents to push their cheeks behind the incisors in order to close the entrance to the throat when they are gnawing and permits them to select what they wish to swallow.

Numerically, the rodents contain more species than any other mammalian order and so are highly successful in evolutionary terms. Indeed, nearly half of all mammalian species are rodents. To give you some idea how successful they are, you can ponder the fact that if there are 250 million people living in North America, there are probably *tens of billions* of rodents, maybe even trillions, and the same is true for most other continents.

An assortment of spiny mice, a species unrelated to the house mouse.

By the time you are at the genera level, the members are all very similar indeed, but are still obviously separate breeding populations. The lowest full rank in animal classification is that of species. It is identified by adding a name to that of the genus. In the case of the mouse, the species is *Mus musculus*, derived from the Latin word, *Mus*, meaning "mouse", and *musculus*, meaning "little mouse." There are numerous identifiable sub populations (subspecies) of mice, and the house mouse is one of them. It is identified from others by having a third name, in this case *domesticus*, added to its species name. The closest relations to the house mouse (other than other mice species and

Mice are found throughout the world and occupy just about every possible ecological niche. The order Rodentia is divided into many families, 35 of which are extant and which contain some 350 or more genera. In these families are to be found all of the Old World mice and rats. The ancestors of the domestic mouse are classified as members of the family Muridae. This family is divided into more than 100 genera, making it the largest mammalian family on our planet.

Above: A long-tailed field mouse (*Apodemus sylvaticus*) tends to its grooming ritual. **Right:** Contrasting sharply with the wild form is the typical white mouse of the pet hobby. Photo by Michael Gilroy.

rats) are hamsters and gerbils, then guinea pigs, chinchillas, squirrels, gophers and many other well known animals. Rabbits and hares are not, as is commonly thought, rodents, but are placed in a related order known as Lagomorpha.

MOUSE FEATURES

The general shape of the mouse is known to virtually everyone, and we have already discussed its prime teeth, the two pairs of incisors. Its other teeth are comprised of 12 molars, three pairs in each of its upper and lower mandibles. There are no deciduous (milk) teeth in mice as there are in cats, dogs, and humans. The digits in mice are 4-5, meaning four toes on the front feet and five on the rear. Its long tail may contain up to 32 vertebrae. The female mouse (called a doe)

normally has five pairs of mammary glands.

The wild coloration of the mouse is, of course, agouti—a blend of black, brown and yellow hairs. The fancy mouse kept as a pet may have one of over 500 combinations of colors and hair types, though only a small percentage of these will normally be seen, even at a large mouse exhibition. In terms of its longevity, a mouse can live up to about five years of age,

An exercise wheel is a worthy addition to the mouse quarters's furnishings. Photo by Michael Gilroy.

though two to three would be a more typical average. Its breeding is discussed in the chapter on this subject, so here it need only be said that few other mammals can rival it in the potential number of offspring a female may produce over her lifetime.

The eyesight of a mouse is not especially good, but its sense of smell is acute. Although it is traditionally regarded as a nocturnal species, a fact that its eye size would support, it may, nonetheless, be very active during the daylight hours. Its dawn, dusk, and nocturnal activities are survival strategies. Even so, millions

An exercise wheel is a worthy addition to the mouse quarters's furnishings. Photo by Michael Gilroy.

of mice are still caught when they do venture out because their natural enemies have developed the ability to hunt well in the dark. It is not thought that mice can see colors because they possess no color-sensitive cones in the eye. They see things in shades running from black through white.

the mouse can detect things about its environment from them. Some hairs may also serve as sensitive vibrissae, though they are not as stiff as the whiskers.

The social organization of mice is typical of many non-predatory groups and is based on the "scatter" principle of survival. In this

Having a large surface area in relation to its body bulk, the mouse can lose heat by air to surface interfaces, so it has no need of sweat glands. Should it become very hot, it will, of course, pant. Its whiskers are long and sensitive. Apart from being able to touch things with them, the whiskers may also be able to sense vibrations in the air. Thus

method, thousands of mice may live in a colony; and should they be attacked, they all scatter in various directions. The hope is that the predator may not be able to fix on a single prey as there is so much activity going on around it as it attacks; each mouse hopes it will be its fellow that is the unfortunate victim. Within the colony, mice live in family groups

The considerable size difference between a mouse and a gerbil illustrates why the two species cannot be kept together. Photo by Michael Gilroy.

It is believed that the domestication of the mouse began in China. Photo by Michael Gilroy.

in which there will be a dominant male or female, a number of females and a number of immature males. As the family grows in number, so fighting breaks out, and young males and females will leave to start their own families or join other small groups. A distinct hierarchy is formed within families and groups. This is essential for the success of the group, as

it is in most other animals, including humans.

HISTORY OF FANCY MICE

It will never be known for certain exactly when the mouse first became a household pet or the subject of specific study, but it is generally felt that the credit for setting it on the path of domestication goes to the Chinese. It is known that white spotting and albinism were evident in mice in China by about 1100 BC. White mice are mentioned by many early historians dating from Greek and Roman times. We have to progress to the 17th century to hear of the appearance of the self black and to the 18th to read of the chocolate and the lilac strains.

However, as with nearly all other domestic pets, it was not until the 19th century that the mouse fancy really began to take off. During that century there was an explosion in the popularity of keeping pets and in the development of many unusual varieties or colors.

Walter Maxey, an Englishman, is credited as being the Father of the Fancy. His interest in these tiny rodents seems to have begun about 1877. As a result of his breeding and activities, the National Mouse Club was formed in England in 1895, and his name lives on in the mouse show cage known as the Maxey.

As more and more people began to take up the keeping of mice, it is not surprising that color mutations began to appear as the 20th century got underway. At that time, Gregor Mendel's theory of genetics was beginning to gain impetus, and the mouse became the chosen animal for genetic experiments. It was the first mammal to demonstrate Mendelism (in 1902).

The fancy mouse, like the canary, was essentially a pet of the working class, and it prospered as such until about the 1950s. At that time people's interest began to turn towards more exotic animals, such as hamsters, chipmunks, and gerbils, which were newcomers on the pet scene. The fancy mouse began to disappear from pet shops, though it remained a popular exhibition animal with dedicated fanciers. In recent years, the mouse, as well as the rat, has enjoyed something of a revival and is once again seen in pet shops in large numbers.

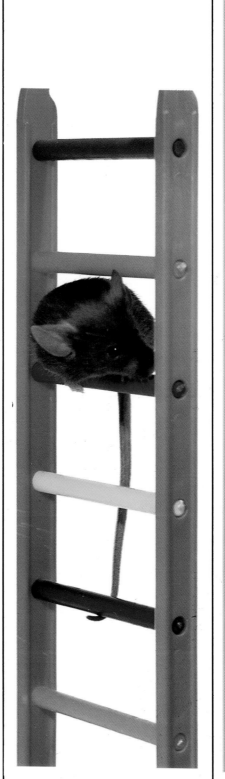

Cage toys are appreciated and utilized by the active, intelligent mouse. Photo by Michael Gilroy.

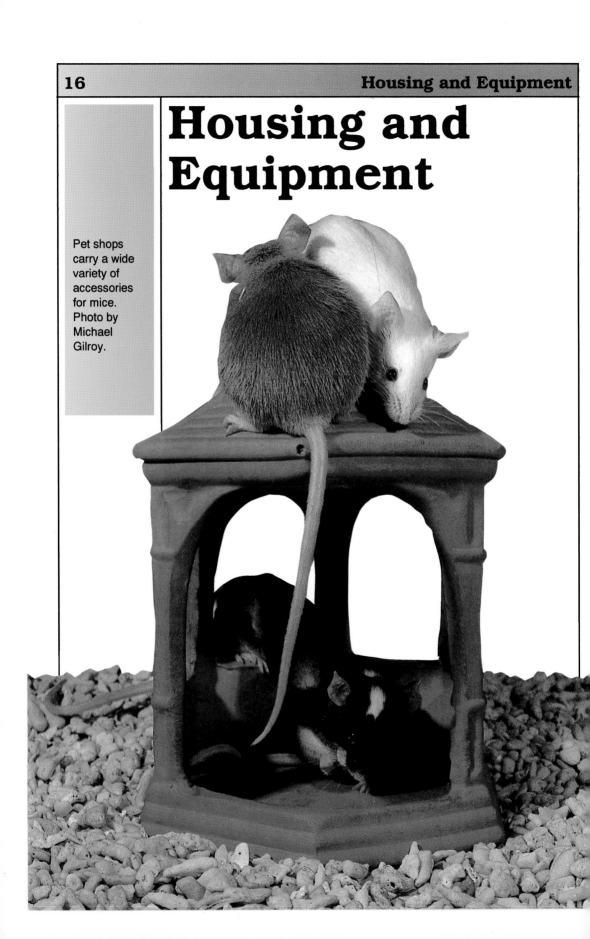

Housing and Equipment

Pet shops carry a wide variety of accessories for mice. Photo by Michael Gilroy.

The type of housing you supply to your mice will reflect your own thoughts on what is and is not acceptable. It will also be influenced by whether or not you plan to keep only a few mice as pets, or whether you wish to set up a breeding stud. The factors that influence any person's ultimate choice of accommodation are the cost, the space available, how easily it can be cleaned, and how suitable it is for the mice.

In respect of the last point, I would have to say that some of the housing commercially available for pet mice is lacking—on par with those terribly small cages still used in some zoos, and in which you see lions, tigers, and bears treading out a pitiful pacing of their few feet of space. There is no need for the pet owner to supply such unsuitable housing, because it does not cost

A black and white mouse. Photo by Horst Bielfeld.

The pet mouse has a unique charm all its own. Photo by Michael Gilroy.

much money to supply a home that reflects modern concepts on captive animal accommodation. Pet shops carry a wide array of small-mammal housing from which you will be able to choose.

COMMERCIAL CAGE OPTIONS

The small all-metal cages that are available for mice have two disadvantages, apart from their size. Metal is a cold surface, so it is not an ideal choice, and it rusts very quickly. Much better are those made of plastic with chromed metal bars. The traditional hamster cage is even better as it affords greater space. However, mice may be able to escape from it unless metal gauze is placed over it until they are too large to squeeze between the bars. The hamster tube systems that are available represent an attempt to provide small rodents with housing that is more interesting.

These attractive units can be arranged in a variety of ways, depending upon the ingenuity of the mouse owner. Additionally, they are priced quite moderately.

An alternative means of housing is via one of the inexpensive plastic aquariums that come complete with hoods. You can add an extra safeguard with a sheet of metal gauze or fire screen wire. The larger the aquarium the more suitable it is as a home for your mice. Aquariums are easy to clean, provide for excellent viewing of your pets, and provide better scope for furnishings than do traditional mouse and hamster cages. A large old aquarium of the metal-frame type would be cheap because aquarists are replacing them with more modern units, so may sell their old aquariums at low cost.

HOMEMADE CAGES

If you are handy and have the time and money to invest, you can construct your own housing for your mouse pets.

I will not give any suggestions of sizes other than to say make it as large as you can— preferably in length, as this gives you greater scope to furnish it. Height is, however, useful as it allows you to create two or more levels for the mice to explore. You can make it in laminated wood with a wire mesh front, in wood with a glass or Plexiglas

Mice are active, inquisitive little animals that can amuse themselves for hours on end. Photo by Michael Gilroy.

A group of satin mice at play in their breeding pen. Photo by E. Jukes.

front, or totally in glass or its plastic equivalent. With regard to the latter, the modern rubber bondings available from pet and aquatic stores mean you can construct a really impressive looking unit. If wood is used, laminated laminated wood is used, it should be a hardwood that has been well coated with a non-lead gloss paint.

If wire is used in any part of the construction, be aware that a hole size of 1.25 x 1.25cm is large enough for baby mice to

wood is the best choice because it is easy to clean, does not absorb urine, and is more difficult for the mice to gnaw on. If a non- escape through. Given this fact, use screen wire, or lay two layers of wire weld over each other so they half the hole size. If wood

small entrance hole on one side, located 2.54cm (1in) above the base. The hole should be just large enough for the mice to clamber through. If it is made of wood, it will give the mice something to gnaw on, thus distracting them from trying to gnaw on the walls of the cage—should they happen to be made of wood. The nesting box could be fitted above floor level with a small ramp leading to the cage floor.

The top of the cage should be hinged so you can open it for cleaning purposes and removal of the mice. It can again be made of Plexiglas, wood, or a mesh fitted onto a

is used, the walls of the cage can be lined with thin-sheet Plexiglas. This offers extra protection and is easier to keep clean.

In terms of general design, the cage should be simple in its shape in order to make cleaning easy. It should feature a nestbox in which the mice can sleep. This can be made as a separate unit that is simply placed into the cage and thus easy to remove and clean. It will consist of a cube or rectangle with dimensions of roughly 13x13cm (5x5in) floor area and a height of 10cm (4in) or a little more. When this is filled with hay or a suitable nesting material, it will thus be warm, dark and cozy. It should feature a

Two of the basics in cage furnishings: the exercise wheel (left) and the feed dispenser (below). Photos by Isabelle Francais.

wooden frame. Alternatively, it can be a lid that slides into position. In the all-glass or Plexiglas cage, you must make provision for air circulation via a number of drilled holes that can be featured high on the side walls, in the lid, or in both. If you

much-needed exercise when they use them. Mice will appreciate different levels to explore so build a ramp system on which they can run up and down. They also like moving through tubes. Your pet shop carries these entertaining devices in a variety of styles, including those that are transparent, thus allowing you to watch the mice as they travel

A duo of pet mice investigating mini bales of hay. Floor covering may be wood shavings, shredded or granulated paper, or hay. Photo by Michael Gilroy.

wish the holes to be of a size that the mice could, in theory, clamber through, should they be able to reach them, the answer is to cover them with perforated zinc sheets.

CAGE FURNISHINGS

In a large cage you have excellent scope to provide the mice with amusements. A popular item is the exercise wheel. Mice, like many other small mammals, enjoy these devices immensely and get

through them.

A few small rocks and pieces of bark will provide an interesting play area for them. You could add a few branches, some dried leaves, and moss, which will give the cage a much more natural look than the customary Spartan floors of most cages. Used cotton bobbins (the wooden type) are other items that the mice will play with and, like the branches, give them something to gnaw on, which is important to all

rodents. If you want to provide your mice with a really super home, install small fluorescent blue night-time lighting. This allows you to watch them when it is dark in the room—a most interesting aspect of keeping nocturnal critters. Once you have seen a really well-planned mouse house that is of generous length (93cm (3ft) or more), it really does make the average mouse cage look rather small! I well recall many years ago (early 1950s) standing in London Zoo totally fascinated by what seemed an enormous mouse village they had built. Although I was only a child, it totally changed my thinking about the housing of any pet animal species. It illustrated just what can be done with a little planning and imagination.

FLOOR COVERING

The choice for covering the floor is sawdust, wood shavings, shredded paper, granulated paper, or hay.

Sand or soil is not recommended, the former because it is abrasive, and the latter because it may contain the spores of pathogens. Hay can be somewhat questionable because it may contain fungal spores that are likely to burst open if the shavings are less absorbent than sawdust, but do not cling to foods as much. The granulated papers are fine. Do not use the wood wool used as packing. You can purchase synthetic materials for the nesting quarters. These are recommended as they are

The breeding setup can be as large or as small as your interest dictates, but cleanliness should always be the watchword. Photo by E. Jukes.

hay is used as bedding—where it may become damp due to the urine of the mice. Sawdust should be of the white softwood type as this is more absorbent than the darker colored hardwood types. Check that it is not from a chemically treated wood as this can be toxic to your pets if eaten—which is almost inevitable. Wood hygienic and cozy. Line the nesting base with sawdust or shredded paper first.

BREEDER CAGES

The mouse breeder cannot afford to have enormous cages, so small breeding boxes or cages are used. These are about 38x20x15cm (15x8x6in) minimum, the measurements quoted being length, width, and height. They should contain a divider in which there is a small entrance hole, the divider creating a nesting compartment. The latter can take up about one third of the length. By having a removable slide it will be easier to clean the box. Those made of plastic and chromed wire are the best because they will not absorb the urine of the male. Molded aquariums are another possibility as they are relatively inexpensive, easy to clean, with a secure mesh top. If you keep a number of mice for breeding purposes, give them due consideration in relation to their need to have an interesting life. It is not difficult to arrange your breeding room such that you have two or three large exercise areas for the mice to enjoy on a rotational basis. They may be large aquariums or exercise runs that are covered in mesh and contain a few diversions, such as tread wheels and tubes, as already

These show cages are much too small to house a mouse except for very brief periods. Photo by E. Jukes.

and have a good depth so the mice cannot escape from them easily. They should, however, be fitted discussed. Apart from giving them some means of amusement, such runs will also keep mice fit, and fit mice will produce more vigorous offspring.

placed on shelves, which can be of wood, or of the angular metal types that can be pur-chased as units and can be

THE BREEDING ROOM

You may have a spare room in your home that can be used for your breeding program, or you may prefer to purchase a suitably-sized shed. It should be light and well ventilated but should be sited where it will not become too hot during the summer months. The breeding cages are

bolted together. The room should be well insulated so it retains heat in the colder months. Some form of heating will be found

Above: An example of the albino "laboratory" mouse. Photo by Dr. Herbert R. Axelrod.
Right: A neat, well-organized breeding area. Photo by Michael Gilroy.

beneficial for you, as much as for the mice.

If you can supply water, sewer, and electricity to the room, so much the better as this will certainly make the daily attention to chores more pleasant. Cover windows with mesh so you can leave them open during the hot months, and be sure no direct sunlight will focus on any of the cages, thus making them too hot. Food containers should be of the airtight type so there is no risk of the food in them being eaten or contaminated by mice—the wild sort! Ensure that the breeding room has ample working surfaces and that the floor area is open so it is easily cleaned and does not allow hiding places for unwanted mice, rats, snakes, or other potential predators.

Among the appliances you should consider featuring in the room is an ionizer. This will remove

Mice appreciate the security offered by snug hiding places. Photo by Michael Gilroy.

These two mice have established a snug nest in cedar chips. Note the very young "pinkies," visible among the chips. Photo by Michael Gilroy.

pathogens from the air. It will also keep the smell of the bucks down to a minimum, if it does not eliminate it altogether. This appliance comes in many models and sizes and is economical to run. If you live in a hot climate it will be worthwhile investing in some form of cooling system, be it ceiling fans or an air conditioning system.

You should always stock a number of spare cages or aquariums so that the mice can be placed in them during cleaning operations.

You should also invest in a hospital unit or make one yourself.

Another consideration for the potential breeder is a quarantine facility.

The final comment in respect of housing is that it must, of course, be kept very clean. At a minimum you will need to do this once a week, depending on the size of the accommodation. You will need a stiff and a soft handbrush, a suitable scraper (such as the small ones used by house decorators), plastic bowls, and plastic trash bins. If you have wooden cages, they should be repainted on a regular basis, and you should keep your eyes open for any signs that the mice may be gnawing holes in them. You can seal any such potential sites by nailing aluminum strips over the holes. However, if at all possible, it is best to use glass or acrylic materials for the housing.

Stock Selection

The way in which you go about stock selection will reflect the purpose for which you are keeping mice: simply as pets or for establishing a breeding nucleus from which exhibition and color strains can be developed. However, for whatever reason the mice are kept, the first priority is that they are healthy. Given the relatively short lifespan of a mouse and its small size, protracted treatment of illnesses is invariably not cost-efficient, which makes it even more important that you start off with healthy examples. We will therefore look at this aspect first and then consider the selection of breeding stock.

HEALTHY MICE

When you are looking to purchase any form of livestock, it is prudent to form an opinion on the seller before all else. The conditions under which the animals are kept is your first and most important guide as to the likely health, and indeed quality, of the stock. If you are unimpressed by the conditions you see, then have no

Mailing tubes make perfectly acceptable, though decidedly temporary, mouse tunnels. Photo by Michael Gilroy.

second thoughts—seek another supplier. The points you should be looking at with respect to mice are the following:

gnawed parts of it, it will be impossible to properly sterilize and the potential source of pathogenic (disease-causing) build up. No seller should be using housing that has clearly passed its effective life. The metal

Right and opposite page: Mice on a tightrope. The antics of these animals point out their natural agility; keep their quarters securely covered! Photo by Michael Gilroy.

1. Are the premises of a generally high standard of cleanliness, or are there sacks or boxes of seeds, oats, and other foods exposed to flies, wild mice, or any other form of potential contamination? Are the shelves and other surfaces clean or are they covered with dust? Is the floor clean? Is there any strong odor? Wherever a number of animals are kept there will normally be some small odor but it should *never* be overpowering.

2. In what condition are the cages or other accommodations? Housing that is made of wood is especially susceptible to the ravages of wear and can be difficult to keep clean. If the mice have

bars on cages should not show evidence of rust.

Aquariums used as housing should not be dirty. Check the lower few inches, against which is where the mice will normally stand up. This area should only have a few marks from that day on it, not be encrusted with dirt that has been there for days, or even weeks. The floor covering should be clean, not excessively soiled with fecal matter, or damp from urine.

3. Food and water containers should be well

filled and clean. They should not be cracked or otherwise damaged—further sources of bacterial colonization.

4. The housing should not be overstocked. The number of mice in a given

the mice run around so you can note that they have no impediment to their movements. There is a genetic condition that causes mice to run in circles. Such mice are called "waltzers" and should be avoided.

size of accommodation should be such that they have ample room to run about. If they are cramped, they will tend to be fighting a lot.

5. There should be no obviously ill or injured mice mixed with healthy stock. Good husbandry should involve checking all stock on a daily basis. When a seller does not have time to do this, he has too much stock and should have reduced the numbers.

If you are satisfied with the conditions under which the mice are being housed and looked after, it is reasonable to suppose that the seller is the sort who would only offer fit and healthy stock to you. Even so, you should know how to assess a healthy mouse yourself. Begin by watching

Mice that are seen to jump a great deal are also undesirable. This may be yet another genetic problem—though it may also be indicative of stress. Either way, you do not need such a mouse.

If you are looking for breeding stock and see waltzers, you should seek another seller because others of the stock that do not exhibit the condition may well be carrying it in their genotype and so can pass it on to their offspring. Of course, in a pet shop situation, the stock may have come from numerous breeders, so other mice on view may

These self-colored mice (above) and the pair of pieds below display the lush, glossy coats of the healthy animal. Photos by Michael Gilroy.

should be free of kinks, again a point of quality rather than health. The coat of a mouse should be immaculate. It should have a high gloss to it, and there should be no areas of missing fur or any indications that the skin has any lumps or abrasions. The whiskers are long; and if any animal is noted with very short or almost no whiskers, it is likely it has been housed with a whisker-biter. If you are selecting breeding stock, you are again advised to proceed cautiously because the culprit might well pass on this trait to its offspring. The one without the whiskers is not the problem, it is finding the whisker biter that is!

Inspect the belly to see that the skin is in good condition, and examine the

not be related to a waltzer.

Once you have found one or two mice that appeal to you, they can be inspected more carefully. The eyes and nose should be free of any form of discharge, the eyes large, round and sparkling. The upper incisors should just overlap and touch those of the bottom jaw, thus ensuring they will wear evenly as the mouse gnaws. If the teeth are not aligned correctly, they will continue to grow and cause problems for the mouse when it is eating.

The ears should be as free of wrinkles as possible—this being a point of quality rather than one of health. The tail

anal area to be sure it is not congealed with fecal matter or stained, either state of which would indicate a problem. Inspect the feet to see that the skin is healthy and that there are no ulcerations or swellings. These could indicate foot rot, but this condition will only be seen where conditions are unhygienic. If all is well you can assume the mouse is a fit and healthy specimen.

SEX AND AGE

If you are purchasing mice as pets and do not wish to breed them, it is important that you purchase *only* females. I say mice, because it is recommended that you keep at least two, which will be company for each other. Mice are gregarious creatures so it is inconsiderate to force them to live in isolation. Females are the better choice because they are virtually odorless. The urine of the males is rather strong and is used as a scent marker, so even with good husbandry they will generate a musty scent—though from one or two specimens this will not really be offensive.

Above: If you are interested in mice as pets (and not breeding them), it is best to keep a pair of females. **Below:** Mice appreciate wooden objects to gnaw on, but beware of toxic paints! Photos by Michael Gilroy.

Plastic cage toys will outlast those made of wood by a considerable margin. Photo by Michael Gilroy.

Females are also more sociable with each other. Young males who have never bred can live in harmony, especially if their accommodation is of generous proportions, but should they begin fighting they can inflict severe wounds on each other. In small cages, one male may continually bully another so purchase only females if they are to be pets.

Mice are easily sexed from a young age—within a few hours of being born—so determining sex should be no problem by the time you are looking to buy them. In the female the anal and genital openings are close together, while in the male there is a much greater distance between these orifices. You will want to purchase young mice because of their rather short lifespan. Unfortunately, once they reach maturity, which is within weeks rather than months, it is difficult to assess age.

When you are purchasing pet mice, it is better if the pet shop or breeder maintains the sexes separately. If not, by the time you purchase a female there is every possibility she will already be pregnant. The female can produce offspring once she is five or six weeks of age. This is not recommended, but it is almost inevitable if the sexes are kept together.

SELECTING BREEDING STOCK

The potential mouse breeder must be much more demanding with respect to the stock purchased. For one thing, it is essential you know something about the genetic background of the stock you acquire. If not, you could waste valuable time and money finding this out by trial and error matings. The first thing you should do is to visit a mouse exhibition. This will give you first-hand knowledge of what the various colors look like in the flesh. Further, at a show you will see far more varieties than you could hope to see at any one other location. You will also be able to study the winners—and the losers— and so begin to understand what the word *quality* means in mice.

You will need to obtain the standards of mice as laid down by the ruling hobby association of your country. Study these in respect to exhibits at shows, and do talk to as many breeders as possible. You are strongly advised to study basic genetics as this is very important in mice— which are the most studied animals in the world in terms of their genetics. The many photographs in this book will give you an appreciation of some of the hundreds of color combinations that may be seen in these pets. Once you have determined which colors appeal to you, it is simply a matter of locating a breeder who specializes in them and has a reputation for producing quality stock. Try to locate a breeder who lives in your locality because you may need to discuss different breed aspects and may well need to purchase more stock at a future date. You are advised to begin with stock from one breeder, not from a number of them. This will enable you to progress with more certainty over their 'type' than if you start crossing lines that have achieved their physical excellence with differing genes.

It is essential that the commercial breeder has maintained detailed records of his breeding program so that he can sell you stock of known genotypes in relation to the colors seen, or being carried, by the individuals you purchase. You will, of course, get what you pay for, but, fortunately, even quality mice are not expensive when compared to other pets.

As far as the number of mice you initially start with is concerned, this is, of course, dependent on the sort of breeding room facility you have invested in. It is unwise to start out with too many mice; there

The hand-tamed mouse—the desired goal of the casual mouse keeper. Photo by Michael Gilroy.

are a number of reasons for this.

1. You may decide that breeding mice is not for you, so it is better that you have only a limited investment in them until this decision can be reached. Very often beginners start off with a rush of enthusiasm that wanes within the first year.

2. The initial stock may not prove to be of the quality you had hoped for. You may thus have to upgrade it.

3. It is better to keep things on a low-key basis while you are learning about mice in a practical manner. This course of action also gives you time to ponder the available colors. You may have a change of heart once you are actually underway, so it is easier to change if only a few of the initial colors (or coat varieties) have been purchased.

With regard to colors and varieties, don't be too ambitious in the numbers of them that you keep. It is far better to specialize in one or two than to try and propagate lots of them and achieve success in none of them.

Although mice are among the least expensive of pets it is nonetheless important that their selection be given plenty of thought. This is because they do breed rapidly, so maintaining a good collection may be just as costly as if you had purchased expensive birds, hamsters, or other more expensive animals. The difference between mice and other small pets is related to their initial cost—not their subsequent upkeep, which might be very similar. If you invest in the best breeding stock, you should get the best prices for quality youngsters. It costs just as much to feed inferior-quality mice as it does high-quality ones.

Feeding

Feeding mice is probably easier than feeding any other pet because mice are so accommodating in their feeding habits. There are, in fact, few foods they will not eat, which is why they have been able to establish themselves in situations where other creatures could not survive. This said, if you want your pets to live a long and healthy life, you must monitor their feeding regimen just as you would any other animal.

ASPECTS OF WET AND DRY FOODS

There are thousands of different food types, but they can be divided into three or four categories based on their constituent values. In the broadest sense, foods can be divided into those that are high in moisture content, such as fruits, greens, fresh meats, and

Above and below: Feeding bowls should be easily cleanable and wide enough to prevent tipping and scattering feed about the cage. Photos by Michael Gilroy.

A field mouse in its natural habitat. Wild mice are too nervous and high-strung to be confined as pets.

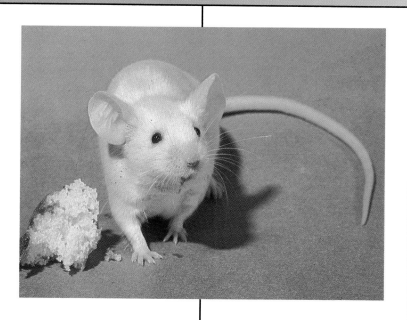

vegetables, and those that are not, such as seeds, dried fruits, and the like. A dried food will have the advantage that its percentage of constituent values will be much higher than with a wet food; in other words it will represent a highly-concentrated form of providing the major food constituents. When dried foods are given to pets it is most important that water is available to them on a 24-hour basis.

If wet foods are supplied, the amount of the food given, in terms of gross weight, will be much more because most of the food will be composed of water. If a mouse eats a lot of wet foods, it will drink less water, but the latter should still be supplied on demand

because you cannot be sure what the mouse's water intake needs may be as an individual. This is dependent on many factors, such as the ambient temperature, the amount of metabolic water produced from the oxidization of foods eaten, and from such matters as the sex of the animal, its

COMPLETE FOODS

In laboratories, mice are invariably fed on a dry matter diet (pellets), plus water, and they survive well enough on this. However, the reason they are given such a regimen is the need for feeding to be practical, easy, and controllable. With dry pellet foods scientists are

Millet is normally thought of as food for cage birds, but mice certainly won't refuse it! Photo by Michael Gilroy.

age, and the amount of fluid lost from the body (urine, milk and respiration). To ensure that your mice are receiving a balanced diet, it is generally advisable to supply them with foods from both the wet and dry categories, plus the constant availability of water.

able to determine exact quantities of given constituents that the mice eat, because the mice are unable to make a selection of individual items. This is important to the scientist, but it does not mean that the mice prefer to eat such a diet. Indeed, when they have a choice, they will always prefer to select from a broad range of foods.

Nutritional scientists may well know most things about the value of differing food items, but they do not know it all, so you are advised to treat so called 'complete' diets with a degree of suspicion. By all means use them, because they are carefully formulated, but do not use them to the exclusion of other items. Those other items just may contain ingredients not yet identified, and that may prove very important when they are. There is also a psychological and social importance to feeding that is not always given its due consideration. It may affect that difficult-to-pinpoint condition known as stress.

THE MAJOR FOOD CONSTITUENTS

The three important food constituents are carbohydrates, proteins, and fats. Additionally, vitamins and minerals are required, though they are not actually foods in themselves. Finally, water is the other vital component of a healthy diet.

Above and left: Your mouse's basic diet of pelleted food can be supplemented with a variety of seed-based treats. Photos by Michael Gilroy.

It is not a good idea to put food directly on the floor of the mouse quarters as the occupants can soil it with their droppings. Photo by H. V. Lacey.

Carbohydrates: These are the ingredients that provide most of the energy used during muscular activity. They are sugars in various forms of complexity and are the least expensive of any food items. Examples are oats, maize, many seeds, and, of course, all byproducts of them, such as bread, biscuits (cookies), and breakfast cereals. Once a mouse has reached physical maturity at about 6-9 months of age, its basic food needs will be primarily carbohydrates.

Crushed oats and foods such as maize and bran, together with any breakfast cereals, should always be available for your mice as they form the basis of the menu. Various hard breads, preferably whole grain, are another rich source of carbohydrates.

Placing the bread in the oven on a low setting for a few minutes will harden the crust even more and will satisfy your pet's gnawing instincts. (Be sure to break up the bread into small pieces.) When soaked in water or milk and then squeezed to remove excess moisture, it will provide an excellent wet food that can be offered by itself or as the basis of a mash.

Seeds that are very rich in carbohydrates are white and yellow millet, canary seed, and wheat. They all contain 58% or more of these compounds. All seeds will, of course, contain carbohydrates, but some, rape and maw seeds for example, contain only about 12%, more or less. Dog biscuits are a useful source of the compound and are often enriched with some vitamins and minerals.

Proteins: These are the building blocks of the body and thus essential to pregnant does and to their young. The muscles of the body are mainly composed of proteins, which are the most numerous components after water. The most obvious source of proteins is meat, whether red or white, and fish. Plant matter has little protein, but seeds, such as peanuts (unsalted), linseed, sunflower, pine nuts, and rape, all have values of 20% or more. Other rich protein sources are milk, eggs, cheese, dried lentils, and beef extracts.

The proteins of animal origin are important because those from plant matter do not contain all of the amino-acids, from which proteins are made, to meet the needs of mice. In the wild, mice would eat insects, worms, and eggs, as well as carrion, in order to meet their animal protein needs.

These various foods can be given in a number of ways. For example, eggs can be scrambled, or they can be boiled and chopped into pieces. Egg yolk can also be part of a mash. Seeds can be given in small dishes, or they too can be included in mixed mashes. The latter can contain virtually any foods, as long as they are all chopped into tiny pieces and well mixed. A small amount of liquid, be it water, milk, or a beef extract, can be poured onto the mash to hold the ingredients together. The mash

The bread served to your pet needn't be bakery fresh, but it should not show any signs of mold.

Above and right: The variety of mouse food is almost limitless, thus ensuring that your mice never need have a boring diet. Photos by Michael Gilroy.

should not be mushy, but rather moist. The advantage of mashes is that the mice will be less selective, so they will take items that you know are good for them but that they might not take if given on their own. Also, medicines can often be sprinkled onto mashes if the need arises.

Fats: These complex compounds are often found in association with proteins, or by themselves, as in fish oils, butter, and lard. They are extremely rich sources of energy (more so than carbohydrates and proteins), but an excess of them is not good for mice as they will affect the absorption of other food items. Further, they can cause obesity. They are an important element of foods because they are responsible for making them palatable. They are essential for transporting compounds around the body in the bloodstream—and, of course, for providing the muscle and skin with protective insulation. Other than those mentioned, rich sources of fats are seeds such as peanuts, sunflower, pine nuts, linseed, and rape.

Fats quickly go rancid once exposed to the air or higher temperatures, and in this form they can be dangerous. This so, when items such as butter or fish oils are added to mashes or other foods, it is important they be removed if the mice do not eat them within a relatively short period of time.

Vitamins: There are many vitamins known to humans. They are all important to mice, with the

are the fruits and green plants. Among those recommended are dandelions, carrots, apricots, spinach, and beet greens, all of which have high vitamin A values.

exception of vitamin C, which the mice can synthesize within their bodies. In fact, mice can manufacture a number of other vitamins as well, so only some of them are essential. However, you need not worry unduly about which can and cannot be synthesized if you supply a varied diet. By so doing you will ensure the mice obtain all of those needed. Vitamin-rich foods

Apples, grapes, and even potatoes will also be enjoyed by your pets.

However, try a range of fruits and vegetables in order to see which your mice enjoy best. Hay is, of course, a very valuable food for mice, and it is normally supplied for bedding, so it has a double value. Make sure it is fresh and dry, never moldy, because in the latter state it is

West African pygmy mice eating a meal of rice and fruit. Note how tiny they are compared to the mice on the opposite page.

potentially very dangerous. All greenfoods and fruits must be washed before being offered to your mice as they may contain residues of toxic pesticides. Their useful life is short once given to the

This homemade mouse mix consists of oats, sunflower seeds, and dog food. Photo by E. Jukes.

mice, so those uneaten after a few hours should be removed and discarded.

With regard to fruit, and especially to green plants, be careful how much you supply. An excess can easily cause the condition known as "scouring." This results in acute diarrhea. If you are unsure on how the mice you purchased were fed, it is best to offer greenfoods in small amounts at first, and then build up slowly so the mice have time to adjust to these foods. This approach holds true for any untried item added to the diet.

Minerals:
Minerals are such items as calcium, phosphorous, iron, copper, sodium, iodine, and other elements. Within a varied diet, all of them will be contained in satisfactory amounts, so need not be given as supplements. The possible exception is calcium, which is required in larger quantities by

pregnant and nursing does. This element is essential to good bone development, so supplements of milk or powdered calcium are often given. However, the ratio of calcium to phosphorous and other elements is important. Therefore, it is essential that the mice are receiving, and eating, a varied diet when extra calcium is given. Otherwise the calcium may not be absorbed and could create problems.

STORING FOODS

All foods should be stored correctly if they are to retain their full values. Dry foods, such as seeds and grain, are best kept in sealed containers in a cupboard. Fruits and vegetable matter should be kept in refrigerators and be well thawed before being fed to the mice. Bear in mind that vegetables that are frozen must be kept at certain temperatures if they are to retain their value. This can vary from item to item, so check the recommendations supplied with your freezer. Mashes can be made in bulk and stored in the refrigerator so you can take out the amounts needed on a daily basis.

BULK PURCHASING

The pet owner with only a few mice will find it economical to purchase packages of mixed dry foods from the pet shop. Those that are proprietary brands are probably fortified with vitamins; those prepared

Above and below: White mice, in various poses of romping and recreation. Photos by Michael Gilroy.

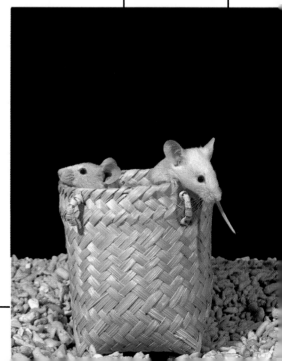

by the pet shop will not be, but they will work out less expensively. Rabbit pellets are suitable for mice as a concentrated dry food. Breeders will find it more economical to bulk purchase their foods as individual items, such as oats, maize, bran, seeds and so on. However, do not buy too much at once because not only is it more difficult to store, but also it will not be as fresh as if you were to purchase somewhat smaller quantities on a more regular basis.

FOOD CONTAINERS

There are many small food containers sold for mice and other small rodents. They range from the open types to the automatic seed and water dispensers. The larger seed dispensers, with wide apertures, will hold grain such as oats, but some breeders prefer to scatter dry foods so that the mice have to search for them among the cage floor litter. If open feeding trays are used, the best are those made of earthenware (crock) as they will not topple over as the mice lean on them. Water is best given in dispensers. There are numerous small models available for the likes of mice, hamsters and gerbils. Again, heavy open bowls can be used but will tend to get soiled with sawdust and other materials. Water must be changed daily, and run the tap for a few seconds before filling the containers. If the water in your locality is

Right and opposite page: Two of the many forms a small mammal cage toy can take. Be sure that the material and paints used in cage toys are non-toxic! Photos by Michael Gilroy.

Feeding

very hard or treated with chemicals, it may pay you to install a purifier or purchase bottled water for your pets. You might be surprised what effect the quality of water can have on small creatures such as birds and rodents, especially in relation to the quality of the feathers and fur.

WHEN TO FEED

It really doesn't matter at what time of the day you feed your pets, the main point being that it is best if it is carried out at the same time. In this way your pets will become familiar with your schedule—they will look forward to it. Dry foods should always be available to them in one form or another. It is also a good idea to record the foods you're supplying so that when foods are added or withdrawn you are better able to assess effects. This will be more important to breeders who can test new foods on some of the stock in order to make comparisons with that previously supplied.

VACATION FEEDING

It is obviously better if a friend or relative can feed your mice when you are away. However, unlike cats and dogs, mice can be left for up to five days without feeding being personally supervised. To do this you must be aware what quantities they eat over a 24-hour period and likewise with the water. It is then a case of supplying quality dry foods in sufficient quantity to last— as well as water. Offer them more than you think they will eat and include a small apple or the like.

The problem with leaving your mice to their own devices is that if one should sicken the day you leave, it may be in a bad state or dead by the time you return, so do this only if there is no other option. Very often a breeder-friend will cover for you.

Breeding

The breeding of mice is a fascinating side of the mouse fancy, but one of its greatest advantages can also be its biggest drawback unless you manage your stock very carefully. Mice are extremely prolific producers, making even the proverbial reproduction of rabbits seem modest by comparison. Given this fact it is vital that, from the outset, you give consideration to both your accommodation facility and how you will dispose of the surplus stock that could arrive at an alarming rate.

Probably more so than with any other pets, the mouse breeder must be a well-organized person—otherwise chaos will quickly ensue. The most important aspect is that the sexes must be separated as soon as possible, thus ensuring that litters are produced only when you want them. With regard to the selling of surplus stock, this can be done in a number of ways. If you become an exhibitor, a number of promising mice will be sold to other exhibitors, or to those just entering the fancy as you did.

Pet shops may take a number of well-marked or nicely colored youngsters, but keep in mind that you cannot always rely on this means to market surplus mice. A less appealing market for surplus stock is to those who keep snakes and other reptiles, or

Closeup of female mouse genitalia. Photo by Michael Gilroy.

but should not exhibit any major faults. What *is* most important is that the seller can show you detailed records of their ancestry.

You need stock from a line that has proven vigor, which means its litter size is good and the offspring have a good health record. The strain should have no known genetic defects, such as the waltzer genes.

As far as the age of the stock is concerned, it should be young but old enough so that it is

Left: External genitalia of the male mouse. Note the greater distance between the anus and the urethra. **Below:** A successful breeding program requires starting out with sound, healthy stock. Photos by Michael Gilroy.

birds of prey. Obviously, such people will feed the mice to these animals as a food item. If this latter market does not appeal to you, then you must ensure you limit the number of offspring so you can dispose of the surplus as pets or breeding stock.

OBTAINING STOCK

As with the purchase of any other kind of pet, take your time in making a final decision.

It is important that your first mice are sound and typical members of their particular variety. They need not be show winners possible to assess its physical state (say at about 3 months or a little older). The peak of a mouse's breeding period will fall between the ages of 4 to 12 months. After the latter age the doe can still produce litters but the number of offspring will tend to decline. You do not need to purchase equal numbers of bucks and does because the male can mate with many females over a given period of time. With this in

mind, it is wise to invest more cash in a few quality bucks. They are then able to perpetuate their genes via the higher number of females initially purchased.

RECORD CARDS

From the outset you should prepare record cards for each of the mice retained for breeding. You should also keep on file details of all matings and their results. There are many recording systems. You may use cards, books, or a word processor, and organize the actual details in a suitable form. The record of the individual mice should show their parent's number, color, and source (if not bred by you). It will then detail their number, sex, color, age, and hair type. It may

also carry details of their major virtues and faults, their genotype, as far as this is known, and such matters as their health record, longevity, number of offspring produced over their lifetime, and in how many litters. Any prizes won can be noted on the records.

In the patterned varieties you may even draw a rough of this on the reverse of the card, or attach such to the record card. Some breeders will even photograph their stock so they have a good visual record of individuals. All of these details will make future matings easier to decide on. They may also help you trace faults, or genetic problems, should they happen at some time in the future. The more detailed the records, the better. Never commit details to memory, because it has been proven many

fertilized if a male is present. The doe will accept a male for 12 or so hours, after which another 4-6 days must pass before another mating will be possible.

The gestation period, that time the egg develops within the doe to the point the youngster is born ranges from 18-21 days.

Riding herd on an active bunch of four-day-old babies. The hair color is just becoming evident.

times that the memory is an unreliable recording system where detail is concerned.

BREEDING DATA

Mice are able to breed once they are four weeks of age. The female's short estrus period cycles every 4-6 days. At this time the doe will ovulate, meaning shed ripe eggs that can be

Exceptions above or below that period are possible. The doe will be capable of re-mating within hours of giving birth to a litter, though this is not recommended. The size of a litter can vary tremendously because it is influenced by so many factors. They include the strain of mice and the age of the female. The age of the male has virtually no influence on litter size, the sperm simply being units of genetic information. They are not, like

the eggs and embryos, affected by the physical state of the doe and her blood, which are intrinsically linked to the offspring.

However, a typical litter will number about ten youngsters, though twice this number could be produced by a prolific doe at the peak of her reproductive life. The doe has ten teats with which to nurse her offspring, which are born blind and naked. The hair color is apparent within a few days, while the eyes open at about the two-week mark. The teeth erupt around day ten and develop steadily from that time. The youngsters are weaned from their mother's milk at about 3-4 weeks of age, and they are capable of coping with soft foods from

Below: A handful of squirming, newborn "pinkies." Photo by Michael Gilroy.

Below: Mother mice will move their young if disturbed too often. Photo by Michael Gilroy.

Right and opposite: The newborn mouse is a tiny, helpless creature, hairless and blind. The eyes open at about two weeks of age, at which time the mouse can begin sampling solid foods. Photos by Michael Gilroy.

about week two onwards, coinciding with the time they are able to see. The ears of recently-born mice are small and lay close to the head. They begin to grow at a fast rate when the youngster is about five days of age. By the time a baby mouse is 16-18 days old it is a miniature adult.

BREEDING CONDITION

This term applies to all potential breeding livestock. It relates to the general condition and preparation of any given pair for the rigors that are always a part of breeding. It is especially applicable to the female, who, of course, bears the entire physical strain involved in carrying and nursing the offspring. She must be in superb condition, never obese or ill in any

way—nor in the process of recovery from an illness. The male must be in similar top shape. If you have any doubts about either, wait for a few weeks. In the weeks that precede the actual pairing you should slowly introduce more protein foods into the diet of the doe and increase the calcium content so the developing embryos will not be short of sustenance. The high-protein diet must be continued throughout the nursing period, then slowly returned back to the non-breeding level.

BREEDING PROCEDURE

The first and foremost advice with regard to breeding is that it is not recommended that you allow very young mice to breed. They should be physically mature, which means about three months of age. If they are not mature, a

great strain is placed on the body, especially that of a female, and this will adversely affect her subsequent growth.

The female should be taken to the male's quarters, otherwise her strong territorial instincts may result in her fighting with the male. Some breeders place the two in a neutral cage, returning each to their own quarters once the female is seen to be pregnant. It is also advised that maiden does, or unproven bucks, are paired with a proven and thus experienced partner. It should be obvious whether or not a doe is pregnant by the twelfth day onwards, and once this has been determined the buck should be removed to his own quarters. It is not a case that he would savage the offspring but that he would mate the female again as soon as a litter has been born, which is undesirable.

Two or more females may share the nesting quarters, assuming that it is large enough. This is beneficial in a number of ways. It minimizes the number of breeding boxes needed and makes feeding an easier chore. Should one female die or become ill, her babies will still be looked after by the other mother(s). Should one female have a large litter and another a small one, the nursing duties will be evenly divided between the two does. The offspring will also benefit from the fact that if one mother is out of the nest feeding, the other

A healthy black mouse romps unconcernedly in its owner's palm. Avoid holding mice over heights as an unexpected leap may end in injury or escape. Photo by Michael Gilroy.

will probably remain to keep the youngters warm—an important point with mice.

However, this shared motherhood is only practical if you have mice of differing colors, coat types or patterns. You must be able to identify the offspring of each mother, otherwise your breeding records will not be reliable!

REARING BABY MICE

how many are sound and healthy and so on. Over the first two days try not to disturb the nest too much, though there are two schools of thought on this matter.

On the one hand, if you do not check the nest daily you will not know if the babies are progressing as they should. Conversely, if you disturb the female too much, she may kill her offspring, this being a

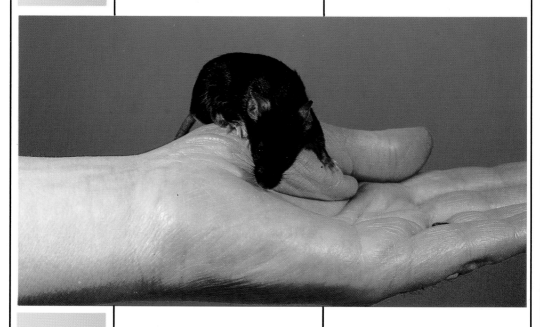

Once the doe has given birth to a litter you should count the number of offspring and inspect the nest. Any deformed offspring will have to be removed and destroyed. Try to inspect the nest while the female is away from it feeding. Record the date of birth, number of young,

natural defense mechanism. Your decision must be based on your need to gather information about the offspring (such as daily weight gain) and what you know about the character of the female. The maiden is normally much more nervous than the experienced mother so

A pied mouse. Photo by Horst Bielfeld.

An assortment of one-month-old mice. Photo by Michael Gilroy.

more likely to panic if disturbed. She may, in any case, kill some of her first litter, but thereafter the arrival of babies will not disturb her.

Mice are excellent parents so unless there is an obvious problem you

will need to do no more than ensure the babies have sufficient food as they grow and that the nest never gets cold. If there is plenty of bedding, it will not; and the risk is even less likely if the breeding room is maintained at a reasonable temperature (not too hot, but always above freezing).

In the event that you were to find newly-born offspring looking pale pink or even bluish in color, remove the breeding box to a warm room or hold the youngsters in your hands for a few moments in order to try and revive them. The

mother may be spending too much time out of the nest or she may simply be a poor mother, a fact that should be recorded on her record card. Never breed from any mother, regardless of how good she is as a mouse, if she does not rear her young as she should. While her offspring can easily be fostered out, this is a poor policy that merely makes things worse as you progress.

Parenting ability is an inherited trait that can be passed on via the buck (from his mother) as well as from the doe. Do not always assume, therefore, that the mother's strain is the problem one—check that of the buck as well.

REARING PROBLEMS

Cannibalism is not uncommon in mice but usually there is a good reason for it. It may be the result of a nutritional deficiency through stress or fear or it may have genetic links. It may also be the result of unhygienic conditions. For example, a massive parasitic invasion of the nest could prompt a doe to desert it or to kill all the babies. As previously mentioned, first-time mothers can panic and destroy some or all of their offspring, but this usually corrects itself at the next litter. When the problem occurs too often to be chance, you must analyze each of the potential causes cited.

SELECTION

Once the youngsters have been weaned at about 3-4 weeks of age, they are best placed into sex groups so there is no chance that the females will quickly become pregnant. You then need to assess the stock very carefully in order to decide which mice will be retained for future breeding and exhibiting and which should be sold. Although, in theory, you should be just as rigid in your selection criteria regardless of sex, in reality you need to be especially so where bucks are concerned. This is because you will not wish to keep as many bucks as does, so those that are retained really should be outstanding and not just adequate.

Mice, like any other form of livestock, can change as they grow. A super youngster may be less so by the time it has matured. A well marked, or colored, specimen may mature to be of less, or better, quality than your original hopes.

What you must do is to ensure that your system of selection is consistent and well thought out in relation to your needs. This means it should be reviewed periodically in order to move the emphasis from one aspect of the mice to another as each character is improved. Regardless of how you grade the mice features, health and vigor should always weigh heavily in your priorities.

A 12-day-old mouse. In a few days, its eyes will open. Photo by Michael Gilroy.

Mice Varieties

Above: A fit
and healthy
mouse. (Note
the very
glossy coat.)
Photo by E.
Jukes.
Below: A
mouse with
Dutch-type
markings.
Photo by
Michael
Gilroy.

While in dogs, cats, and rabbits there are a varying number of distinct breeds, each having its own unique appearance, the situation is quite different in mice. In these animals the appearance is unaltered but the colors and coat types may be different, so they are called varieties.

The main variety groups are: 1. Selfs, 2. Marked or Patterned, 3. Tans, 4. Silvered, 5. Coat varieties.

The tans are in fact patterned varieties, but it is convenient to regard them as a group. This also applies to the silvered. The various hair types can be seen in any of the first four groups, so you can have a longhaired, or rex, or satin in any of the colors and patterns. That is, in theory, because hair type is not linked in any way to color. In practice, some color combinations and patterns are not seen in all of the hair types simply because they have not as yet been developed. It can be added that there are a number of known color and coat mutations that are not generally available in mice because they are either linked to undesirable traits or have no benefit to the mouse fancy as a whole. For example, in the latter group, there are *mimic genes*. They are genes that create a similar appearance to an existing and well-established mutation. Were they to be introduced in numbers, the result would be a great deal of confusion. They usually exist in research laboratory strains. We will look at each of the groups and, in the case of the colors, discuss the more popular members of them.

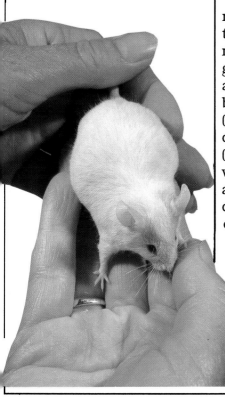

SELFS

A self is a single-colored mouse. Most will breed true, while others are the result of combinations of genes. Popular examples are red, fawn, cinnamon, black, blue, chocolate, dove (lilac), cream, silver, champagne, and white (albino, or black-eyed). It is very important that selfs are literally that—single-colored—and should exhibit no hairs of another color. In reality, this is very difficult to achieve because some other colored hairs are almost invariably present. For example, blacks may display a few yellowish hairs or some pink in their nails so only

Above: A pair of bi-colored mice. **Left:** An obviously pregnant mouse. Photo by Michael Gilroy.

through rigid selection for the color over many generations is the desired state reached. A good self is a most impressive mouse.

A point of importance in respect to the gene that creates red (which is genetically yellow) is that it is one of several

genes that are lethal in mice. This means that when in a pure form the offspring do not survive. All red-based mice (such as fawns, cream, and sable) carry this gene. If they are bred to their own or related colors,

the resulting litter size will be 25% smaller than a normal litter.

MARKED OR PATTERNED

Under this general heading will be found

Outward signs of good health in a mouse: a glossy coat and bright, clear eyes. Photo by Michael Gilroy.

as seen in other color varieties of mice, such as the chinchilla. There are a number of colored agoutis, such as the blue, and the argente.

Sable: This pattern is produced when black or very dark, brown hairs are intermingled with those of the basic red color. The hairs on the back are very dark, and the pattern becomes more red as it progresses down the flanks of the mouse. There are numerous sable color possibilities, such as the blue, the chocolate, and the marten

mice that display two or more colors in various combinations but which are not within the tan or silvered groups. It is a large group with many very attractive varieties.

Agouti: This is the wild coloration of the mouse, but it has been refined over the centuries to be a more golden color. The coat comprises bands of black, brown and yellow, which, with the overlapping effect of the hairs, produces the famous ticked effect seen in many

Above and below: There is a wide variety of colors and patterns from which you can choose. Photos by Michael Gilroy.

(chinchilla), but not all are striking and thus not as popular.

Broken and Even: These two coat patterns are both variations of the gene that also creates the Dutch variety. The gene is called

wild creatures (due to its excellent camouflage properties). The belly of the agouti mouse is also ticked, not white or light colored as in other animals, or indeed

white spotting, or piebald. It is totally unpredictable in its expression, so breeding any of its variants is as much a matter of luck as judgment. A broken pattern is one in which there are numerous patches or spots of color spread in an uneven manner over the coat. One of these patches must be on one side of the nose. The even pattern must display as many patches or spots of color as possible but they should appear on both sides of the body. The spots can be any color, so you can have a black broken or a chocolate even and so on.

Dutch: This pattern is the same as seen in the rabbit. A colored rear end plus a colored patch around the eyes, contrasted against the rest of the body, which is white. The Dutch pattern can be seen in many colors though black, blue, and chocolate are especially pleasing. Any variety that involves the white spotting (pied) gene is difficult to produce to a good standard. The result is that many will fall below exhibition level. The only policy a breeder can follow is to mate the best marked animals that he has.

Rumpwhite: In this variety the rear one-third of the mouse's body should be white (including legs and tail) while the rest should be colored. The line of demarcation should be sharp. The gene responsible for this variety is prenatally lethal so two rumpwhites should not be paired to each other. Otherwise, a quarter of the theoretical litter will die before or shortly after birth. The recommended mating is rumpwhite to a self variety.

Himalayan: This pattern is the same as that seen in other pets, such as the rabbit (for whom it was named), guinea pigs, and cats.

Its feature is that the points of the body (face, feet, ears, and tail) are colored, while the rest of the body is white or a lighter shade of the points. It is unusual in that it is thermo-sensitive, meaning that it is affected by the ambient temperature. In cooler conditions the points are a little darker than when it is warm. It is possible to have many color variations of the Himalayan, though only a few have been

Eye color is another consideration in the selection of your mice. Some people like the dark-eyed varieties while others opt for red-eyed animals, as shown here. Photos by Michael Gilroy.

Below and opposite page: Mice on wheels. These little "vehicles" are impractical for use as toys in smaller cages. Photos by Michael Gilroy.

developed in the mouse at this point in time. The darker chocolate Himalayans are known as Siamese in the mouse fancy.

Variegated: This is a rarely seen variety. It has a color pattern streaked or brindled with white. The variegation can range from an almost white mouse with a few flecks of color to an almost colored mouse with flecks of white. Spots or patches of color are undesirable, making this a difficult variety to establish.

Belted: In this variety there is a white band that encircles the mid part of the body, the rest being a color. The width and quality of the band are very variable. It is not a popular variety, which is surprising as its equivalent in the hamster is. It is not a variation on the pied gene but rather is the result of its own mutation.

TANS

The tan group of colors has been around for a long time and

consists
of a colored body
contrasting against a tan
belly. The legs and feet are
the same color as the
body. The result is a very
attractive mouse. There is
a significant difference
between quality exhibition
examples and those of pet
quality. The former have a
belly that is a rich even
color, whereas the latter
tend to have a very pale
tan color that improves
only where it meets the
body color.

The body color can be
black, chocolate, dove,
blue, champagne, or
silver—indeed any color
that has official
recognition with the ruling
mouse association.

Fox: This is a tan that
carries the chinchilla gene,
which dilutes the tan color
to white. The result is that
the belly is white, but
there are also white-tipped
hairs on the feet, flanks
and rump. It is a very

striking variety that is
available in black, blue,
chocolate, and other
body colors, though all
are not officially
recognized.

SILVERED
Mice in this small
group of varieties have
silver tipping to their fur,
the tipping extending to
the feet. There are three
levels of silvering: dark,
medium and light. The
recognized varieties are
silver-gray, silver-brown,
and silver-fawn. These
are, in effect, silver-
tipped blacks,
chocolates, and pink-
eyed fawns. A very pale
silver-gray variety is
recognized as the pearl.

COAT VARIETIES
Although a number of
coat mutations are
known in mice,
including one for

Mice at play. Adaptable, inquisitive, and highly intelligent little creatures, mice need and appreciate diversions when kept in confinement. Photos by Michael Gilroy.

coat, but in some instances there would be no advantage in doing so. For example, in many of the patterned varieties a long coat would merely distort the pattern. As a result it is best seen in the self and is most commonly found in whites at this time. Apart from being long, the coat should also be dense and silky. It is to be hoped that mouse breeders never take hair length to the extremes seen in guinea pigs (in the form of the Sheltie and Peruvian varieties).

hairlessness, only three are seen in fancy mice. They are the longcoat, rex, and satin.

Longcoat: In this variety the standard requires the coat to be as long as possible. In the exhibition mouse it is about twice the length of the normal coat and becomes evident by the time the mouse is 3 to 4 weeks of age. It is possible to have any color with a long

Rex: The rex mutation in mice cannot be compared to that seen in pets such as the rabbit, hamster, cat, or guinea pig. It is most evident when the mouse is young, but it looks more like a poorly coated normal as the mouse matures. The whiskers are bent, a feature of the rex mutation, and the coat has a sort of marcel wave. The earliest form of rex was called the astrex, for the mutation known in rabbits and cats. There are in fact at least two forms of rex, one being the result of a dominant gene, the others being the result of recessives. The latter are termed waved, frizzy, and fuzzy, depending on the mutation involved. That they are all separate mutations can be established when they are paired and all normal coats result. This proves the genes must be at differing loci. It is hoped that

in the coming years the rex will improve as a variety.

Satin: This mutation results in a super glossy sheen to the already silky appearance of the coat. Colors tend to be slightly darker than in normal coats. This is because the pigment cells in the satin coat are arranged more closely together, displacing air sacs in the hair shaft.

OTHER VARIETIES

Abyssinian: This mutation, which is very popular in guinea pigs, is

A mouse of the silver color variety. Photo by Michael Gilroy.

known to exist in laboratory mice (though not of the same quality). In this coat type, rosettes of hair form on the body. It may well appear in fancy mice some day.

Tricolored Mice: Three-colored mice are reported from time to time but have never been established. The problem is that they are either mosaics or are linked to genetic defects such as waddling (whereby they cannot walk straight), deafness, and infertility. A mosaic is the result of chemical distortion in the cells, so is not inherited but rather environmental in origin. Mottling and brindling are also mutations that exist in mice but not in fancy mice, due to the defects with which they are associated. However, through the process known as "crossing over" it may one day be possible to separate lethal and adverse genes from those that might add interest to the already enormous range of mutations and recombinations.

This setup looks like fun, but it is certainly not practical as permanent mouse quarters. Photo by Michael Gilroy.

Color and Genetics

In order to really become involved in the breeding of color varieties, it is almost obligatory that you should have a basic understanding of how genes work. They are the minuscule units of coded information that pass from one generation to the next and are the basis of heredity. Genes control not only color but also every physical feature of the mouse, as well as many traits, such as aggression, parenthood, and so on.

Genes are arranged in a linear manner on structures called chromosomes. The latter are found in equally-sized pairs in all body cells, but in the sex cells the chromosomes are of unequal length. The mouse has 20 pairs of chromosomes, and they contain many thousands of genes. When the sex cells are formed, the chromosome pairs divide so that only one will be passed from each parent, thus resulting in paired chromosomes again in the offspring and maintaining the 20-pair situation. From this you will appreciate that each parent contributes half—no more, no less—of its chromosomes, and thus genes, to its off-spring.

Just one of the many mouse color strains available: a recessive pied, wild-colored mouse. Photo by Horst Bielfeld.

The one pair of unequal-length chromosomes determines the sex.

LOCI

The specific site of a given gene on its chromosome is called its *locus* (plural *loci*), and on the opposite chromosome of a pair will be a gene at the same locus and which controls the same feature. There are thousands of loci, and a number of them control color.

MUTATIONS

A mutation is a sudden change in the information a gene imparts. It is not known exactly what causes a gene to mutate, but once it has done so it acts in one of many ways. Genetics is the study of these differing ways. A specific gene can be identified only when it does mutate. It is important that you fully understand the principles of mutation and of differing loci if you are to understand genetics. Let us consider a simple example and work from it.

The wild mouse is an agouti color, this being a mixture of black, brown, and yellow-red. These colors are created by pigments. However, there is not just one pair of genes that controls this color but a number of pairs, and they are situated at differing loci. This is known because of the various mutations that have occurred at them. There are many such is the full combination of the instructions the genes at each locus give that will determine the color. Taking the agouti as an example, the paired genes at this locus (one on each chromosome, remember) both instruct the hair cells to form each of the two basic pigments and present them as the agouti pattern. At the black locus the genes instruct that the black pigment be fully present. At the full-color locus the genes instruct that the pigments (whichever are present) are displayed to their maximum extent.

At the density locus the genes instruct the cells to allow the pigments (whichever they are) to be at full density. Finally, at the pink-eyed locus the

loci, but for our introductory purposes we need only consider five of them because they are very important in creating most of the color varieties seen in mice.

They are not all on the same chromosome, but we will assume they are for explanatory purposes. They are the following:
1. Agouti-locus A
2. Black-locus B
3. Full-color-locus C
4. Density-locus D
5. Pink-eyed-locus P

In considering the color of a given mouse you must bear in mind that it

Right: Blue
Fox color
variety.
**Opposite
page:**
Chinchilla
variety.
Photos by
E. Jukes.

genes tell the cells to be at full pigment strength, which results in a black or very dark-eyed mouse, and the body colors likewise to be at full strength. You will note that a number of these loci appear to be giving the same instructions, which they are, but you will soon see that the manner in which each locus is able to carry out its instructions is influenced by what is happening at other loci.

If a mutation should happen at the agouti locus and resulted in the genes telling the cells not to form yellow-red or brown, but to extend the black, the result would obviously be a black mouse. This would mean that the agouti gene now existed in two forms: one for agouti, and another for non-agouti. A mouse could receive either of these genes from its parents,

depending which type the parents had. They might have two agouti genes, two non-agouti genes, or one of each.

Considering the non-agouti mouse, it is black because all of the other gene loci are unaffected—they are still giving their instructions as normal. If, however, mutations should also occur at any of the other loci, you must consider how they would affect the color. It should also be added that a mutation can happen more than once at a given locus.

Using the agouti locus as a case in point, there are no less than six known mutations at this locus. A given mouse can carry just one of these forms, the same one on each of its two chromosomes, or two of them, one on each chromosome, but no more than two. The alternate form of a given gene is called its allele, so non-agouti is the allele of agouti, and vice versa. If this concept of numerous loci and numerous mutations at a given loci is understood, we can progress to look at other aspects of gene action (still using the agouti as our example).

AGOUTI X NON-AGOUTI

In order to calculate expectations from matings it is convenient to apply letters to represent given genes. We will give the agouti gene a capital *A*, and its alternate form, non-agouti, a lowercase *a*. Both are given the same letter to remind us we are talking about alternate genes at the same locus. The reason agouti is given a capital letter will be apparent shortly.

If an agouti mouse is mated to a non-agouti (black), the result will be 100% agouti offspring. Let us show this in a formula:

AA x *aa* = *Aa Aa Aa Aa*

The agouti mouse has one *A* gene on each of its two chromosomes. The non-agouti has one *a* gene on each of its chromosomes. Each parent can pass one of its chromosomes, and thus genes, to its offspring. In this instance, each parent has only one possibility in what it can pass, thus the offspring must have an *A* and an *a*. Their genotype is *Aa*. Their phenotype (what they look like) is agouti, because the *A* gene is more powerful than the *a* in terms of its ability to express itself. It is said to be dominant to the *a*, which is said to be recessive. The parents are called *homozygous* for their color because both of their genes are for the same color. However, their offspring are *heterozygous* for color (non-purebreeding) because they carry a gene for each of the two possible colors. They are said to be agouti split for non-agouti. This is written as agouti/ non-agouti.

Exhibiting Mice

Above: An
argente doe.
Opposite:
Regular
handling will
help to
prepare your
mouse for
the rigors of
a show.
Photos by E.
Jukes.

If you plan to be a breeder of mice it is reasonable to assume you will also be interested in exhibiting. This pursuit has many advantages to a breeder, the most obvious being that it enables you to see how your breeding program is progressing in comparison to that of others. If you consistently fail to garner prizes in competition, this would suggest that your concept of what constitutes quality is in need of revision—or your mice are in serious need of being upgraded.

Another advantage to the exhibition side of the fancy is that it brings you into contact with those who share your interest in mice. From such contacts long-standing friendships are often established. Further, you will gain much knowledge by discussing any problem areas with those who have a long experience in the hobby. At a show you will be able to see, and probably purchase, quality stock. Later on you will be able to sell your own stock to other breeders and novices, assuming you have built a reputation for producing sound examples. The whole atmosphere of a large mouse show is quite fascinating, and you could easily get 'hooked' on it.

Shows for mice can range from the small informal affairs organized by local clubs to the large national shows, which are

The tail of the show mouse should be at least as long as its body. Photo by E. Jukes.

sponsored by the ruling mouse association of your particular country. Sometimes mouse shows are held in conjunction with those for other rodents, such as rats, hamsters, and gerbils.

THE EXHIBITION MOUSE

It is impossible to convey in words what the exhibition mouse should look like so we can only consider basic guidelines. Quality is in the eye of the beholder, and in the case of the mouse exhibitor this means the judge! This illustrious group of men and women are as subject to personal preferences as anyone, and the written standards for mice are, of necessity, flexible to allow for variable interpretations by the judges. Were this not so, the same mice would win all the time, and there would be no fun in exhibiting. You must, therefore, study the standards applicable to your varieties, and then note the mice to which judges give the awards. Finally, study those mice that did not win.

In this manner you will build up a mental picture of how the standard relates to quality and why the average mouse is just that, rather than a winner. Never be afraid to admit your lack of knowledge, and ask a judge (if she or he has the time after judging) why this or that mouse was better than another.

The first essential of an exhibition mouse is that it be in superb condition, and this is only possible if its diet and living conditions are first class. It must not be skinny, nor fat; the coat should glisten with sheen. This can only come from within, not by externally applied lotions and the like. In any case, the use of artificial aids in order to improve the look of a coat are against competition rules. This does not mean you cannot shampoo your mice, but you cannot use anything on the coat that will in any way alter its color in order to make it appear better than it actually is.

The exhibition mouse must possess good color for its variety. This means no tan or white hairs on a black mouse, and so on, according to the color. If it is a patterned variety such as the Dutch or rumpwhite, the lines of color demarcation must be clear. The placement of marks or colors should be as near to the standard's requirement as possible. The tail of any show mouse should be at least as long as its body, and it should have a good thick root that tapers nicely to the tip, rather than an even thickness along its length. The ears should be large and as free from wrinkles as possible, while the eyes should be large and round, without bulging. The whiskers should be long, unless in a rex-coated variety. A quality mouse will, of course, have a very supple body with no tendency to

A show-quality mouse will have a body that is nicely proportioned. Photo by Michael Gilroy.

A judge's eye-view of the Maxey show cage—compact, easy to access, and portable. Photo by E. Jukes.

be unduly "roach-backed," nor should its back show a sag. With regard to size, it is not a case of being as large as possible but being of good size, providing the proportions are pleasing.

PREPARING THE SHOW MOUSE

Other than ensuring prime condition is maintained, there is virtually no preparation required for the exhibition mouse. A groom with a silk cloth will give the mouse that extra polish, which will be maintained between shows if its bedding is of high quality hay. Care must be taken prior to shows as to what foods are offered your mice. For example, supplying beets to a white or light-colored mouse would not be the wisest thing to do if a show was pending; the juice could easily stain the coat. Dark sawdust or shavings are much more likely to stain a coat than those from white woods.

With long-coated mice, as well as those with normal coats that are of a light color, a bath a few

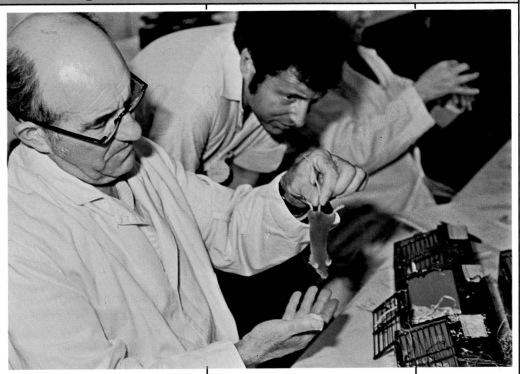

days before a show may be worthwhile if the mouse has become soiled in any way. This must be done with care. Ensure that no water gets in the ears or eyes, and be equally sure that any shampoo is well rinsed out. Otherwise the coat will lack luster, may become sticky, and could trigger a skin irritation.

THE SHOW CAGE

Mice must be displayed in a standard exhibition cage called a "Maxey," named for its designer and long-time fancier, Walter Maxey, who died in 1949. There are two designs: one with horizontal bars and one that has a solid front with a circular mesh in it.

The colors are standard, being Brunswick green outside and signal red inside (in Great Britain). You can purchase them from specialist suppliers or make your own to the standards of which your mouse association will supply details. Special traveling boxes are available for carrying one or more Maxeys. The cage should contain clean sawdust, food, and enough hay to keep the mouse warm.

EXHIBITION CLASSES

The classes scheduled by a given show will vary according to the size and likely entry. However, the following is typical of a

British show. If you live in any other country you should check the rules and regulations, though they normally follow the same basic procedures.

Show classes will be divided into the varieties, such as selfs, (i.e., creams, blacks, whites, and so on), patterned (broken, even, Dutch, et. al.) and AOV (Any Other Variety). AOV will cover any variety that has no variety class to enter. The classes will be divided between those for adults and those for mice under eight weeks of age. There will also be classes for bucks and does. There are numerous other classes, such as those for breeders and those called "challenge classes." The latter classes are known as duplicates, and in order to enter them you must also have entered one of the variety classes.

JUDGING

Competing mice are taken to the judge's table in their cages. The procedure is then simply a matter of personal method by the judge, but the following is essentially what happens. The judge will make an initial assessment of the entrants, removing any that are clearly not in the running. Next, of those remaining, one will be selected for

Mouse show contenders are carefully examined individually and often repeatedly before a decision is reached. Photo by E. Jukes.

careful scrutiny. The judge will remove it from its cage and hold it for examination. The next mouse will then be compared with the first and placed ahead of it or behind it in quality. Next, the third mouse is compared with the first two and placed accordingly. By repeating this procedure the judge will arrange the mice, now in their cages, in an order of excellence. The judge may then make another check of the leaders just to be sure he or she is satisfied with the placings.

In challenge classes the first, second, third, and reserve winners of their respective variety classes are all brought together. The class winners are then compared with each other to determine the best overall mouse, and the rest are placed in a descending order. Now the second-best mice from their classes will

Pet quality or show quality, mice are curious little creatures that enjoy investigating their surroundings. Photo by M. Gilroy.

Above: A mouse with Siamese-type markings. **Opposite:** The mouse fancy includes people of all ages. Photo by E. Jukes.

be compared with those already placed. When this has been done the judge will move to the third placed, and then the reserve mice.

By this method it is possible for a mouse that was only reserve in its variety class to beat another mouse that was its class winner. This comes about because it may well be that the overall standard in, say, self-reds, is superior to that seen in Dutch. All four of the self-reds may be better examples of their variety than the Dutch winner is of its variety. This means that a class winner may not get a second look when it comes to the challenge class placings, while a mouse that was only third in its class could beat all of the other class winners—and those that finished second or third in those classes. The section winners will all compete for the Best-In-Show Award. A mouse that was not entered in the challenge classes is not overlooked when it comes to the BIS award and so can still win this award.

The prizes awarded in mouse shows are not as financially rewarding as those in top dog or cat shows, but this in no way lessens the thrill of winning. The singular advantage you have as a mouse hobbyist—over those in the dog and cat fancies—is that you do not need to be the wealthiest person on the block to achieve great success. A superb mouse can be purchased by the average hobbyist, and the reproductive rate of mice is such that you can develop a real strain of mice—an accomplishment dog and cat people talk about but are never actually able to do in reality in all but a few rare instances. Before entering your mice in competitions, you are strongly urged to attend a few shows first and be an active member of your local mouse club.

The Pet Mouse

The mouse is a truly delightful animal and one that was very possibly the first pet to thousands of children over the centuries. It remains excitement rather than intention. Mice will get along fine with other small rodents such as gerbils and hamsters if they have

A 14-day-old youngster. Photo by Horst Bielfeld.

as true today as it was in the past. These are inquisitive little animals, and they also become extremely tame. There are, however, a number of precautions that need to be taken when your mouse is allowed out of its home.

THE MOUSE AND OTHER PETS

If you have pets such as dogs and cats, you must ensure that these animals are never left alone with your mouse when it is out of its cage. As benign as these other pets may be, they are a mouse's natural predators and could easily kill it, if only out of

been brought up together from babyhood. However, caution is advised because the hamster, for example, is essentially a solitary creature and can be belligerent at times. Housing a rat and a mouse together is not a good idea because the rat is so much larger that if things went wrong it could very quickly kill your pet. Simply put, the best companions for mice are other mice.

SAFETY PRECAUTIONS

You must always be aware that should a mouse get loose in a room it may escape under or within furniture or other household items. Should one of the latter be a refrigerator or washing machine, it is not easily moved. Should this situation arise, it may be necessary to lure your pet with food items. Alternatively, if the mouse's cage is placed near the appliance or furniture, the mouse may eventually return to it to feed of its own volition—assuming you have left the cage open so that the mouse can enter it.

You may decide to give the mouse some fresh air and place its cage in the garden for a short period; if you do, be aware that mice can suffer from sunburn so the cage must have a sheltered nestbox in it. Bear in mind that mice are not natural sun-worshipers like you, your dog, or your cat. They suffer when things get too hot. If the mouse is placed in a shady spot, be sure you remain with it as well so it is never intimidated or frightened by cats or dogs peering into the cage.

Supervise your children when they are playing with the mouse because they can easily lose it or hurt it by playing too roughly with it. Teach your children to be gentle and responsible in the care of the mouse and all its needs.

Daily exercise can help to keep your mice fit and healthy. Photo by Michael Gilroy.

HANDLING

Mice quickly become tame, but as babies they are both small and very quick in their movements. They are also very capable jumpers. When you first obtain your mouse and it is placed in its cage, the first thing to do is to allow it to explore and then settle down. Next, you can offer it tidbits through the bars so it can get to know your individual smell. You can then attempt to handle it, being very sure it can see your hand so that it is not startled; in this state it is much more likely to bite.

You can lift your mouse by gently ushering it into a corner of the cage and then taking hold of the root

Above and below: Accessories for the pet mouse of today are durable, attractive, and moderately priced. Photos by Michael Gilroy.

(never the tip) of the tail between your index finger and thumb. Lift it just a little bit and place your free hand under the mouse. Once you have done this a few times the mouse will be quite happy to sit on your hand, and you can carefully stroke it. Eventually, you will be able to lift the mouse up with your hand, but always be very sure you do not squeeze it as this will really put it off being handled. Be very sure children are taught from the outset to hold the mouse with care.

A mouse will happily sit on your hand or arm and will enjoy exploring your body, climbing up your arm or chest and sitting on your shoulder. These are very intelligent little animals if you care to spend the time with them!

Should you ever need to retrieve a less-than-willing mouse from its cage, the best approach is to use a piece of thin hardboard a few inches wide and somewhat longer in length. Place it in front of the mouse once you have cornered it, and he will step onto it if you move the board very gently forward. Once on, the mouse will tend to stay put, unless it is a very nervous individual.

Again, it is strongly recommended that you keep two or more mice so that they provide company for each other. Invest in imaginative accommodations that will occupy and amuse your pets.

Health Care

If you are the owner of a few pet mice, the chances of their contracting a serious disease are much less than is the case with a breeder maintaining many animals. This is because your pets will live in a relatively isolated environment so many risks

incubating a problem or you might introduce an additional pet to your collection that is carrying a disease without showing outward clinical signs. Given these facts, the pet owner should heed the advice given in this chapter, even though most of it is directed at the would-be breeder/exhibitor.

ROUTINE HYGIENE

A great many diseases are passed from one mouse to another simply because

inherent to those who breed and exhibit mice will not be applicable. However, you might purchase a mouse that is already

Typical mouse breeding quarters showing removable top for easy cleaning. Photo by E. Jukes.

the owner was lax on routine hygiene. This shows itself in many ways that you must be especially aware of.

1. When filling food or water containers, always be sure they are placed back in the same cage that they came from and always wash them first; you can number the cages and the feeders that belong to them. Discard any food or water containers that are cracked, chipped, or have passed the point where they can be properly cleaned.

Objects made of wicker or similar material are a no-no for mice. Photo by Michael Gilroy.

2. All cages must be thoroughly cleaned once every week at the least; be sure the corners are given special attention. It is also wise to have a number of spare cages on hand so that by rotation all cages will have a number of weeks when they are not in use.

3. All food items must be fresh and stored correctly. This applies equally to floor coverings and bedding material. Be very particular about the quality of the hay you purchase. That obtained in bales may well have been home to wild mice and thus contain parasites or the spores of fungi.

4. Always wash your hands after handling mice from each cage. Use disposable surgical gloves when handling any mice thought to be ill.

5. Wear a nylon overall when working in your mouse room. It is more hygienic than your jacket or

other clothes, which easily allow parasites to be transported from one place to the other.

6. Do not go directly into your mouse room after you have been gardening; you could transport all manner of problems into the room via your shoes. Always be aware that bacteria and other pathogens must get into your mouse room in one way or another before they can cause problems; you are one of the most obvious ways this can be achieved!

QUARANTINE

A lack of a quarantine period is probably on a par with a lack of hygiene as the main reason why a breeder will be hit with a disease outbreak. Indeed, for a number of breeders who maintain high standards of hygiene, it is surprising that some ignore the value of quarantine altogether. In other instances the quarantine arrangements are unsatisfactory because they are in the same room as the main stock.

A further comment that is applicable to many breeder/exhibitors is that they often do not keep their exhibition stock separate from their main stock. They work on the basis that their stock is healthy but

overlook the vital fact that every time it leaves their mouse room to be exhibited it is placed in a high risk area. It is then taken back to the main breeding room. This is courting disaster—sooner or later.

The object of quarantine is to isolate newly-acquired stock from any other animals in order that it can be screened for possible problems. If a mouse has an illness that was not apparent at the time of purchase, it will have the opportunity to show itself during the quarantine period. The latter should be

A mouse in the process of "tiring" itself out. Photo by Michael Gilroy.

at least 14 days, with 21 being better. During this period you will also be able to carefully monitor feeding habits and adjust the regimen to that followed by you.

In an ideal setup, a breeder/exhibitor will have three areas of operation. One will be the main breeding area, the second the show team area, and the third the quarantine area. The latter should be as far away from the other two as possible. By adopting this approach, you greatly minimize the risk of introducing an infection to all of your stock that might easily wipe out years of careful work and planning. Returning show mice are placed either in the quarantine area or into the show team area. Clearly, this presents the exhibitor with additional set-up and operational problems, so it comes down to just how badly you would be affected if you were to lose all of your prime breeding mice.

Be sure to clean *all* cage accessories on a regular basis. Photo by Michael Gilroy.

KNOW YOUR MICE

Mice are no different from birds, fish, or people in that they are all individuals with their own little mannerisms. Often, a subtle change in behavior may be the only outward sign that a mouse is unwell. The next thing you may notice is the mouse lying dead in its cage. Behavior may take the form of the mouse's eating habits. Is it a dainty feeder or a real glutton? Does it always approach the cage quickly when you bring tidbits or does it hang back? Does it always eat this or that item?

Does it drink a lot or very little?

Any change from the normal pattern of behavior is invariably linked to a specific reason. The animal may

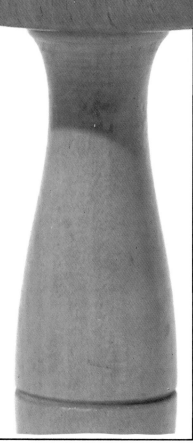

just be having an 'off' day, which all animals have, or it may be the first sign of an impending illness. It is essential that you know your mice on a one-for-one basis. If you do not have the time to watch your mice when they feed, and to spend some time monitoring their behavior, then you simply have too many mice and should reduce your stock.

TAKING APPROPRIATE ACTION

The mouse has a rapid metabolic rate, and this means that an illness can progress very quickly unless prompt action is taken. Conversely, it can

Take time daily to observe your pet's behavior. By doing so, you will be better able to tell when the animal is not feeling up to par. Photo by Michael Gilroy.

recover equally quickly for the same reason. Once you suspect that one or more mice are ill, it is essential that you isolate them promptly for further observation. It is better to

3. Urine or fecal matter is blood stained.

4. Discharge from the nose or eyes.

5. It is sitting in a hunched position and showing no interest in

A young mouse peeks out from the security of a gentle hand. Photo by Glen S. Axelrod.

react to a false alarm than delay in this matter; such a delay may spread the problem to others.

Your decision to take action should be based on any of the following clinical or behavioral signs:

1. Loss of appetite; the mouse is disinterested in its food.

2. It is drinking excessively.

what is going on around it; it is generally lethargic.

6. It has sore spots on its body and is scratching a lot.

7. It has encrustations around its jaws.

8. It has a lump.

9. It has an abrasion or cut.

Once you have isolated the mouse, you should make careful notes on the situation; they may prove important in tracing the cause of the problem. This is as crucial as the treatment because you do not want a recurrence or the ailment to spread to your other mice. There are many questions that you should answer, among them the following:

1. What were the first signs that prompted you to take action?

2. Has the mouse been ill before?

3. Are any other mice showing similar symptoms?

4. Is the mouse a recent addition to your stock? If so, note its source. Was it quarantined?

5. Have you changed the diet of the mouse recently, or the supplier of your foods, or increased any part of the diet?

6. Have you or the mouse recently visited any places where mice may have been ill, such as a pet shop, a show, or another breeder's establishment?

7. Is there any chance that the mouse food may have been contaminated in any way by wild mice, rats, or wild bird droppings?

8. Are there any piles of rotting vegetation near your mouse shed or building—or any forms of garbage that might have become a source of bacterial or fungal colonization?

Depending on the clinical signs you are reacting to, some of these questions will not apply to your particular problem. You have now isolated the mouse or mice and have carefully made notes on the situation. You should also be honest about the state of hygiene that you maintain. If you are less than honest with yourself, then this is a problem with which you are unlikely to make any lasting progress.

Plexiglas or molded plastic aquariums make acceptable mouse quarters (preferably somewhat roomier than the one shown here). Photo by Michael Gilroy.

Index